D1347114

OKE GIRLS
SCHOOL

One Girl School

Jon Blake

Illustrated by Tony Ross

OXFORD
UNIVERSITY PRESS

Contents

1	Save Marnover School	7
2	The petition	12
3	The first day	17
4	Mr Stains takes the register	24
5	Never say 'sandwiches'	30
6	Making publicity	39
7	The Old Marnover Fly	45
8	Marnover School – a school with a future!	53
9	Breaking the law	56
10	Detention	63
11	More problems – and a hairnet	68
12	The inspectors are coming	73
13	A class full of children	77
14	Crisis!	85
15	The secret crypt	90
16	Mum grants a wish	106
	About the author	110

Dear Reader

The story I'm about to tell is completely true except for the following:

1. The ending.
2. The beginning
3. The bit in between

Your friend

Bernie
XX

CHAPTER 1

Save Marnover School

Marnover Village Hall was crammed full of people. Up on the stage was Mrs Whiffy, Head of Marnover Village School, and behind her was a banner: MARNOVER SCHOOL MUST NOT CLOSE. In front of her were rows of angry parents, confused kids and screaming babies. Right at the back of the hall, chewing on a stale bit of gum, looking really bored, was me.

My name is Bernie Lee. That's short for Bernadette, except no one calls me Bernadette unless they want a close-up view of my fist. My mum moved to this stupid village after she split up with Dad. We used to live in Grosshampton, which is a nice big city where the air is ninety-nine per cent petrol fumes. Mum decided it was better to live in the country, so my brain wouldn't get full of poison. Having poison in your brain makes you very poorly and also thick. That's my excuse, anyway.

As I was saying, Mrs Whiffy was up on stage making a speech. She obviously wasn't used to talking to grown-ups and now and again told someone off for looking out of the window. But everyone did as they were told because once upon a time Mrs Whiffy had taught them all and they still seemed a bit scared of her.

'Marnover School,' said Mrs Whiffy, 'has served this village for generations. Marnover School is cosy, comfy, cuddly and *traditional*. But the council says it's too small. The council wants to send your children to Bigtown Monster Primary, which is huge, faceless, fowsty and fifteen miles away!'

There was a howl of protest from the parents.

'I've heard there are sixty-five pupils in every class!' one cried.

'Yes!' called another. 'And some children have been lost for weeks in the corridors!'

'Exactly,' said Mrs Whiffy. 'Which is why we must save Marnover School!'

There was a huge round of applause.

Mrs Whiffy hushed the crowd. 'We need some volunteers to take round a petition,' she said, and explained to the children that a petition was a letter of protest that everybody put their name on.

Mrs Whiffy's eagle eyes scanned the room and, to my horror, fell on me. 'You at the back!' she cried. 'You, chewing the gum!' Of course, Mrs Whiffy knew the names of all her pupils, but I hadn't even started at the school yet. If I had my way I never would.

'I've got a bad arm, Miss,' I said.

'That's all right,' said Mrs Whiffy. 'You only need one arm to carry a petition.'

CHAPTER 2

The petition

So that's how I got my first (unpaid) job in Marnover village. Mum said it was an excellent chance to meet all the interesting local people, and if I was lucky they might give me some local cheese or home-made rhubarb-and-ginger jam.

I sulked for a few days, then I had an idea. What if I kind of, you know, put people off signing the petition? Then, with any luck, the school would close and I'd go to that nice, big modern place in Bigtown after all. Well, it was worth a shot.

I started at Old Appletree Cottage which had a thatched roof, roses round the door and a surround-sound, home-cinema telly in the front room. A woman with a posh voice answered the door. That didn't surprise me. No one seemed to speak in oo-arr country accents in Marnover.

'I'd like you to sign a petition to save Marnover School,' I announced.

'Certainly!' she replied.

'Why should we go to Bigtown Monster Primary?' I said.

'Yes, why should you?' chimed the woman.

'Just because it's got the best exam results in the country,' I added.

'I beg your pardon?' said the woman.

We talked a little more and, funnily enough, she changed her mind about signing the petition.

My next stop was the vicarage, where Mr Fuggles the vicar invited me in for tea and scones.

'I wasn't too keen on Marnover School at

first,' I admitted, 'but when I heard they were going to have a school disco blasting out five hundred watts of bass-booming hip-hop I changed my mind completely.'

'Five hundred watts of *what*?' said the vicar, spraying crumbs all over me. For some reason, he didn't want to sign either. This petition wasn't going well at all.

I decided to call next at Old Farm Road. It's funny they call it Old Farm Road because it's full of brand spanking-new houses. You'd think that would mean there'd be tons of kids for the village school. But the houses are all full of retired people which means they're at least ninety.

I called on a nice old couple in a chalet bungalow.

'Sign the petition?' they said. 'Of course we'll sign the petition!'

'Thank goodness for that,' I said. 'The rest of the village has refused to sign.'

The couple looked at the blank page and frowns crossed their faces.

'Makes you wonder if they know something we don't,' I said.

The frowns grew stronger. 'What do you think that could be?' they asked.

I shrugged.

'Maybe we ought to leave it,' they said.

'Suit yourselves,' I replied.

Yes, I was well pleased with my work on the petition. Only thing was, I was a bit *too* successful. Soon all kinds of rumours were flying round the village. Some parents decided it would be safer, after all, to send their kids to

Bigtown Monster Primary. Then others thought the numbers would be so low at Marnover School, the council was *bound* to close it. So they decided to send their kids to Bigtown as well.

In fact, there was only one parent who was one hundred per cent behind the village school. My mum.

CHAPTER 3

The first day

So there we were, on the first day of term. Mum and me, at the gates of Marnover School. The school was at least a hundred years old and no bigger than some of the new houses on Old Farm Road.

'Please, Mum!' I said. 'They'll kill me if they find out what I did with the petition!'

'Nonsense,' said Mum. 'This school is perfect for you. Small classes, old-fashioned teachers, and no fumes. Your brain will develop by leaps and bounds. Now give your mother a kiss.'

I pulled myself free and marched sulkily

towards the school door. I don't kiss anybody, least of all relatives.

Mrs Whiffy was at the door to meet me. Up close she looked friendlier, with a sucked-out face and crinkly lines round her eyes. She wore a matching grey twinset with flat shoes and stockings as thick as socks. Mind you, she was still the trendiest person in Marnover. 'Welcome, young lady!' she said. 'And you are?'

'Bernie Lee, Miss.'

'Congratulations, Bernilee, you're the first pupil to arrive. Come inside and meet the staff.'

Mrs Whiffy took me through a cosy cloakroom to the school hall. On the left was a table with plates full of cakes and about fifty beakers of squash. On the right were five grown-ups sitting in a semicircle with a carpet in front of them. The carpet was for me. I sat down, all alone, in the middle of it.

'We have a new pupil!' said Mrs Whiffy. 'Her name is Bernilee.'

'Bernie Lee,' I corrected, but no one seemed

to hear.

'Let me introduce my staff,' said Mrs Whiffy. And these were the people she introduced.

MR STAINS

Mr Stains was the Deputy Head. He was an old man with side-whiskers who looked like he'd been trampled on the way to school. Either that, or he'd slept in his suit and then rolled around in a wet garden. He looked dimly towards me with watery-grey eyes and smiled weakly, showing off a very fine set of false teeth.

MISS DORRIT

Miss Dorrit looked like a little girl only bigger and older. She had an Alice band, a pleated skirt and a jumper with little sheep all over it. She gave me a big eager smile and talked to me as if I was about two. I could see she was dying to get out a read-along book and sit me on her knee.

MR ZINN

Mr Zinn was a bit worrying at first sight. He wore a shell suit and thick-rimmed glasses and had a very intense look on his face.

In his hand was a squeeze-ball which he pumped mercilessly. His smile was a sudden flicker, as if his mouth had suffered a small electric shock.

MR TOMSKY

Mr Tomsky was the caretaker. Mrs Whiffy said he was the most important person in the school, but all Heads say that about caretakers. If caretakers are so important, how come they're not paid more than teachers?

Anyway, Mr Tomsky didn't act too important. He just sat there with his arms folded over his beer belly and gave me a matey wink.

MRS FLOSS

Mrs Floss was the school cook. She was hardly any taller than me and looked like a fairground fortune teller, with big, round, gypsy earrings and wildly made-up eyes. These eyes half looked at me and half at each other.

'You look like a stew-and-dumplings type to me,' she said. 'Are you a Scorpio?'

'Gemini,' I replied.

'Gemini, eh?' she said. 'In that case, I'll put in some onions.'

When she'd finished introducing the staff, Mrs Whiffy asked if I had any questions.

'Can we start on the cakes?' I asked.

Mrs Whiffy laughed, thinking I was making a joke. 'We'll just wait for the others,' she said.

Five minutes passed. Mrs Whiffy checked

her watch. 'Oh dear,' she said. 'The others are late.'

Another five minutes passed.

'The others should be here any moment now,' said Mrs Whiffy.

Another five minutes passed. Then another ten. The squeak from Mr Zinn's squeeze-ball was growing louder.

'I really must give an assembly on good time-keeping,' said Mrs Whiffy.

By now it was nearly break-time.

'Do you think I should go home?' I suggested.

A glint of panic came into Mrs Whiffy's eyes. 'Go home?' she spluttered. 'Why would you want to do a stupid thing like that?'

Out of the corner of my eye, I saw Mr Tomsky sliding across to cover the exit door. Time carried on passing.

Eventually it was obvious, even to Mrs Whiffy, that no one else was coming.

'I think we'd better start school,' she said.

'Just with me?' I asked.

'For now,' said Mrs Whiffy.

The teachers discussed whose form I should be in. Mr Stains suggested Mr Stains'. Miss Dorrit suggested Miss Dorrit's, and Mr Zinn suggested Mr Zinn's. I suggested tossing a coin.

'The only solution,' said Mrs Whiffy, 'is that we *all* teach Bernilee.'

'All at once?' mumbled Mr Stains.

'No, not all at once!' snapped Mrs Whiffy, who was getting quite irritable by now. 'We'll take it in turns.'

After a short discussion, Mrs Whiffy decided that Mr Stains should teach me first. Mr Stains had been at the school the longest and, besides, he tended to doze off in the afternoons.

CHAPTER 4

Mr Stains takes the register

My first lesson at Marnover School was the
most tiresome experience of my life. Mr Stains
had had the same routine for thirty-five years
and he wasn't changing it for me. First he filled
out his register, which seemed to take about
half an hour. Then he cleared his throat.
'Before we begin,' he said, 'I'll just take the
register.' Another few minutes passed while his
shaky finger traced down the page.

'Bernadette . . . Lee,' he finally croaked.
(Unfortunately they'd found out my real name
by now.)

'Sir,' I mumbled, rather embarrassed.

Mr Stains looked up and scanned the empty classroom. 'Was that a "present"?' he asked.

'Yes, sir,' I replied.

'Ah,' he said. 'There you are.'

Mr Stains ever-so-slowly penned a little slanting line in the register. It was almost as if he was carving stone.

'Good,' he said. 'That's that over with.'

Mr Stains opened his desk drawer, took out an old ledger and began to read it.

'Now,' he said. 'It's Monday. And that means the lesson is . . .'

There was a loud DRINNNNNG! First lesson was over, and Miss Dorrit was already at the door.

Miss Dorrit wasn't at all like Mr Stains. She perched herself on the edge of her desk, rolled up her sleeves and asked me about ten thousand questions all about myself. All the time she had this big happy grin on her face, except when I talked about living in the city. Then two little frown lines appeared, and she said everything sounded frightfully smelly and rude. 'Anyway,' she said, clapping her hands together. 'I thought we'd start with some *painting*. Do you like *painting*, Bernie?'

'S'alright,' I mumbled.

'I knew you'd like it!' said Miss Dorrit.

Miss Dorrit asked me if I'd like to be paintbrush monitor, responsible for getting the paintbrushes out. I didn't see anyone else volunteering, so I said yes. Then she made me water monitor, pencil monitor and paper monitor. Half-way through this, Mrs Whiffy came in and asked me if she could have a volunteer to carry the tea urn into the staff room.

'Goodness, you are popular!' said Miss

Dorrit, as I staggered back into the room.

For the first lesson, Miss Dorrit said we would make a wall frieze. 'Do you know how to make a wall frieze?' she asked.

'Throw ice at it?' I suggested.

Miss Dorrit was a bit slow on the uptake and didn't realize I'd made a joke.

'No, Bernie,' she said. 'We get everybody in class to paint a self-portrait, then we put them all together on the wall.'

'Excuse me, Miss,' I replied, 'but I'm the only one here.'

'Yes, but the others will all be here soon,' said Miss Dorrit. 'We can add their paintings later.'

I was doubtful but I went along with it. You've got to go along with teachers or they get confused. So I dipped into the paint and got going.

After a while I was quite absorbed. Everything was calm and quiet, except for a sudden high-pitched giggle when Miss Dorrit finally got my joke.

'Wonderful!' said Miss Dorrit when I was done. 'We must take this to show Mrs Whiffy!'

Hmm, I thought. Maybe this school isn't so bad after all. I never got taken to the Head at the last dump.

Mrs Whiffy seemed quite impressed by my painting as well. 'You've got the blotchy red cheeks perfectly,' she said.

'Actually,' I replied, 'that's where I spilled some paint.'

'Oh,' said Mrs Whiffy, rather embarrassed.

'I've just had a wonderful idea,' said Mrs Dorrit. 'Why don't we do a school tea-towel? It would bring excellent publicity and also contribute to the school funds.'

Mrs Whiffy was all for this. Publicity was obviously what the school needed. She had already rung the local paper and was considering hiring a plane to do some sky-writing. 'Do you have any ideas for publicity?' Mrs Whiffy asked me.

I was just about to explain that I didn't have any ideas about anything when the dinner bell rang.

CHAPTER 5

Never say 'sandwiches'

Mrs Floss greeted us with glee in her eyes. The servery was full of steaming trays and she had even prepared a little menu:

MAIN COURSE
A four-ounce, pure-beef pattie served on a bed of lettuce in a plain or wholemeal bap, with a generous serving of finely-sliced and lightly-fried potatoes.
Or
One small deep-pan pizza purchased from a reputable supermarket, with a

generous serving of finely-sliced and lightly-fried potatoes.

SECOND COURSE
Sun-dried plums with short grain rice baked in a piquant creamy sauce.

Or
Yoghurt

APERITIFS
Fresh tap water flavoured with a delicate hint of fruit squash.

'Well?' said Mrs Floss, eagerly. 'What'll it be?'

'Actually,' I replied, 'I've brought sandwiches.'

There was a howl from Mrs Floss and she disappeared from view in the direction of the floor. Miss Dorrit hurried into the kitchen to tend to her and Mrs Whiffy turned to me in horror. 'Didn't anybody warn you?' she said. 'You must never say "sandwiches" in front of Mrs Floss.'

31

It took five minutes before Mrs Floss was back on her feet and another five before the colour was back in her cheeks. After this, I felt I ought to have everything on the menu. That turned out to be burger and chips, pizza and chips, prunes and rice pudding, yoghurt and squash. The teachers sat munching at the next table and Mrs Floss stood right beside me, watching every mouthful with glee.

'Is it to your liking, Miss Lee?' she asked, as I finally forced the last prune down.

'Mm, lovely,' I grunted, trying hard not to spoil things by bringing it all back up again. 'Much better than . . . those square things with bread round them.'

'Excellent!' said Mrs Floss. 'I can see you'll want double portions tomorrow!'

I groaned inside. Pretending to be a class of twenty was hard enough, but eating their dinners was just too much.

The rest of the lunch hour just flew by. Miss Dorrit needed a volunteer to help tidy out the stock cupboard and Mr Tomsky needed a volunteer to flea-comb the school cat. Mr Stains needed a volunteer to take a message to Mrs Whiffy, then Mrs Whiffy needed a volunteer to go back to Mr Stains and find out what the message meant.

I was glad to be kept busy. It kept my mind off the next lesson. The next lesson was games and the teacher was Mr Zinn.

* * *

At one-thirty precisely, Mr Zinn marched out into the playground. There was a ball in his hand, a whistle round his neck and even a little book in his pocket, presumably for taking people's names.

'Come along,' he barked. 'Let's have you lining up.'

I lined up as best I could.

'Today is Monday,' said Mr Zinn, 'and that means five-a-side football.'

'Five-a-side football?' I repeated. 'Won't that be rather difficult, Sir?'

'Who said that?' barked Mr Zinn.

I owned up immediately.

'Ah,' said Mr Zinn. 'Bernadette. I might have known. Always ready with a cheeky answer.'

'I thought it was a question, Sir.'

'And there's another!' Mr Zinn's hand hovered dangerously near his little book. 'We *are* getting off on the wrong foot, aren't we?'

I decided to say no more. As I mentioned before, Mr Zinn was very intense, and a big vein was standing out on his forehead. I was worried his brain might explode.

'Right,' said Mr Zinn. 'You shall be a captain, Bernadette. Would you like to pick your team?'

Yes, it was definitely better to go along with this man.

'OK,' I said. 'I pick . . . me.'

'Good,' said Mr Zinn. 'Now we'll need another captain.'

'You, Sir?' I suggested, hesitantly.

Mr Zinn gave a short, sharp, rather frightening laugh. 'Captain *and* referee? You must be mad, Bernadette!'

Mr Zinn scanned the empty playground, turning a full circle on his heel, his eyes finally returning to me.

'Ah!' he exclaimed. 'Lee! You'll be the other captain!'

'As you say, Sir,' I murmured. 'I pick . . . er . . . me.'

Mr Zinn clapped his hands, took hold of his whistle, and grounded the ball. 'Kick off!' he barked.

I really wasn't sure what to do, but I was determined to try hard at it. At least I had the chance to play footy. At Bottwell, my last school, they said I wasn't good enough to play with the boys. The fact was, I was too good. Especially at fouls. They called me the Butcher of Bottwell and no one would go near me.

I gave the ball a great welly down the playground and chased after it. Then I tackled myself and wellied it back the other way. Mr Zinn watched all this intently with the whistle poised before his lips. I won a corner and took a short one to myself. A goal looked certain but a desperate lunge saved the day. By now Mr Zinn was getting very excited and beginning to shout. Mr Zinn was obviously one of those teachers who has favourites, and before long half the village knew about it.

'Good man, Bernadette! Get stuck in there! No, no, *no*, Lee, it's a football, not a rice pudding! That's it, Bernadette, pass and move, use your triangles! For Pete's sake, Lee, you should be playing with the girls!'

All this had a strange effect on me. When I was playing to the left I really believed in myself and couldn't put a foot wrong. When I was playing to the right I was totally useless. The game was so one-sided it was embarrassing. Afterwards I stood steaming like a racehorse while Mr Zinn gave me some more useful advice about using the long ball, making the extra man and playing in the hole.

'You've done very well, Bernadette,' he said. 'I think we'll give you a shot in the school team.'

I knew this didn't mean very much, but I still couldn't help feeling good about it.

'In fact,' said Mr Zinn, 'I'm going to make you captain.'

The word 'captain' lit up my brain like a neon light. It was my deepest wish come true. I almost wanted to hug Mr Zinn, but not quite. The moment the three-thirty bell went, I grabbed my stuff and raced home to tell Mum the exciting news. Of course, I had to leave out the bit about me being the only pupil. Anyway, there'd soon be lots more pupils at the school now that I'd decided I was staying.

CHAPTER 6

Making publicity

Everyone was so pleased to see me next morning. Mr Tomsky had specially polished his keys in my honour, and Mrs Floss was making exactly the same dinner as the day before, as I'd enjoyed it so much. Mrs Whiffy, however, was looking very tense, and Mr Zinn now had a squeeze-ball in either hand. As nine o'clock came round, there was no sign of any other pupils. Apparently all the kids had hated Bigtown Monster Primary, so the parents were convinced it must be a good school. Marnover School looked doomed.

Morning assembly was a depressing experience. All the teachers except Miss Dorrit were mumbly-grumbly type singers, and I just opened and closed my mouth as usual, hoping no one would notice. Next, Mrs Whiffy gave us the morning talk. Her tone was very serious and she used lots of long words so we knew what she said was important. I have had these words translated so everyone can understand them.

'This morning,' said Mrs Whiffy, 'I have been informed (told) that this institution (school) is to be the subject of an inspection (someone's going to look at it). This inspection is to take place imminently (very soon). If the inspectors find fewer than six pupils to a class, the school will be closed forthwith (right away). All employees (staff) will be given compulsory redundancy (thrown on the dole). Needless to say I am devastated (gobsmacked).'

There was a hushed silence. Mr Stains' lip quivered. 'But what are we going to do?' he peeped.

Miss Dorrit strode to the front. 'Everything

will be fine!' she said. 'We've already started making publicity!' She whipped a tea-towel from her bag. 'I got this idea from Cowsnest Juniors,' she said.

Miss Dorrit held up the tea-towel.

'And here's ours,' said Miss Dorrit.

'I thought we might go down to Upper Dogsbottom,' suggested Miss Dorrit, 'and sell it outside the cattle market.'

Mr Stains volunteered for this job, as he used

to teach some of the farmers during the Second World War.

'I was hoping to have an advert in the sky,' said Mrs Whiffy, 'drawn by a plane. Unfortunately, however, this would cost five thousand pounds, and the school fund only runs to three pounds fifty. So Mr Tomsky has knocked up something rather cheaper.'

Mr Tomsky stepped forward. He was wearing two wooden placards, one on his front and one on his back, with straps over the shoulders. The placards said JOIN MARNOVER SCHOOL – A SCHOOL WITH A FUTURE.

'It's called a sandwich-board,' he said.

There was a gasp from Mrs Floss.

'I mean a . . . an ironing board,' stammered Mr Tomsky. It was obviously the first thing that came into his head.

'But Mr Tomsky,' blithered Mr Stains. 'Won't you find it rather heavy?'

'Oh, *I'm* not carrying it!' replied Mr Tomsky. 'I have the school boiler to look after.'

'Looks like we need a volunteer,' said Mrs

Whiffy.

I began backing towards the door.

'No, not you, Bernadette,' said Mrs Whiffy. 'If you go, we'll have no one to teach. I suggest this is a job for Mr Zinn.'

Mr Zinn did not look happy. 'I am a teacher,' he grunted through gritted teeth.

'Yes, but not for much longer,' said Mrs Whiffy, 'if we don't attract any new pupils.'

Mr Zinn glowered but said no more. The sandwich-board was lowered on to his shoulders and he was sent off to tramp the country lanes from village to village till going-home time.

CHAPTER 7

The Old Marnover Fly

With Mr Zinn out of the way, Mr Stains seemed in a much better mood. He zipped through the register in no more than twenty minutes, then said I could write a story on any subject of my choice.

I decided to write a story about the Old Marnover Fly. Ever since we arrived in Marnover, the locals had been warning us about the Old Marnover Fly. He hung out down by the river, they said, and his bites came up like pizzas. I often pictured him in my head. He was huge and bright shiny green.

In my story, I decided, he would be a friendly fly. I was always getting told off at my last school for writing horror stories, so here was my chance to change.

I started to write but was soon in difficulties.

'Please, Sir,' I asked, 'what do you call that thing a fly sucks through?'

'A proboscis,' replied Mr Stains.

'Pro . . . boss . . . kiss,' I repeated.

'Would you like me to spell that for you?' asked Mr Stains.

'No, thank you,' I replied. 'I think I've got it.'

My story was soon steaming along. I don't know if it was the quiet, or the country air, but I felt really inspired.

I wrote about this kindly old teacher strolling down the fields, then I got all poetic and talked about the dragonflies and bulrushes down by the river and stuff like that.

Then the old teacher leans over the bridge and catches sight of the Old Marnover Fly. The Old Marnover Fly is sitting by his bonfire with a crooked stick and an old clay pipe. He bids the teacher good morn and offers him a toasted muffin. They have this long conversation about nothing, and the sun's sinking over the horizon and everything's going warmly orange.

'Thank you, good fly,' says the teacher. 'Everyone says bad things about you, but I can see you mean well.'

'Good evening to you, and fare ye well,' says the fly.

'Fare ye well also,' says the teacher.

So saying the teacher sets off up the hill towards the setting sun. It looks like it's the end of the film – story, I mean. Then, suddenly, just when you least expect it, the Old Marnover Fly lands with a THUNK on his back and sticks his probosskiss in his bald patch and has him for tea.

Well, you've got to have a shock ending, haven't you? There's always a shock ending.

I know Mr Stains liked my story. A weak smile came to his lips as he began to read it. I may have imagined it, but I think his hand briefly met his eye to wipe away a tear.

Suddenly, however, his smile vanished, his face became slightly green and he hurried from the room, mumbling something about going home. I don't know what upset him. Maybe I spelt 'probosskiss' wrong.

Miss Dorrit was very excited when it was her turn to teach me. She had emptied half the stock room and could hardly be seen behind the coloured markers, rulers, calculators, poster paper, lined paper and graph paper.

'We're going to do a survey, Bernie!' she bubbled.

'Is it easy?' I asked.

'It is for a bright girl like you!' she replied.

I didn't like to disagree with Miss Dorrit, and wondered if she knew I was also captain of the school football team.

'First you need to make a questionnaire,' said Miss Dorrit.

Miss Dorrit gave me a sheet of paper, a clipboard and a pencil.

'Now you need a question,' said Miss Dorrit.

'Such as?'

'Such as . . . "How do you intend to vote at the next general election?" '

'All right then.' I began writing this down.

'It doesn't *have* to be that question,' said Miss Dorrit. 'That was just an example.'

'It'll do,' I replied. I finished writing it. 'Now, who do I ask?'

Miss Dorrit scanned the empty room. A small frown creased her brow. Her perfect lesson hadn't been planned as well as she thought.

'I could ask the rest of the staff,' I suggested.

Miss Dorrit shook her head. 'Mrs Whiffy, Mr Tomsky and Mrs Floss have gone to Old Soxtink to get their photos in the paper,' she said. 'And as you know, Mr Zinn and Mr Stains are also out of school.'

'I could go down the shops and ask passersby,' I suggested.

'Shops?' repeated Miss Dorrit. 'There's only one shop in Marnover. And that's closed on Tuesday.'

Things were looking pretty bleak. But all was not lost.

'Miss Dorrit,' I asked brightly. 'How do you intend to vote at the next general election?'

Miss Dorrit was not at all prepared for this question. She blushed slightly. 'Well,' she began, 'there doesn't seem to be much to choose from. All the parties are much the same.'

My pencil hovered. Miss Dorrit thought a little harder. 'I shall probably vote for the Monster Raving Loony Party,' she said, 'as a protest.'

I wrote this down, and that was the end of the survey. Miss Dorrit then explained how to use the results to make a bar chart. This is what my bar chart looked like:

Survey of how we will vote	0	1	2	3	4	5
Labour						
Conservatives						
Liberal Democrats						
Monster Raving Loony	■					

Next, I had to multiply the results by forty million, because forty million people had the right to vote. From this I could work out exactly how many seats each party would win at the next general election.

The results were as follows:

LABOUR PARTY 0 seats

CONSERVATIVE PARTY 0 seats

LIBERAL DEMOCRATS 0 seats

MONSTER RAVING LOONY PARTY 659 seats

Yes, the world certainly looked different when you lived in Marnover.

CHAPTER 8

Marnover School – a school with a future!

After school that afternoon I decided to go home the long way. The long way took you down through some fields to the river, where our old friend the Old Marnover Fly would no doubt be waiting. Sometimes I liked to scare myself like that.

It was a nice bright autumn afternoon and I was almost starting to like the country. Everything was quiet and twittery with no one bugging you. There were grasses and fungi and berries and not all of them were deadly poisonous. There were paths through the hilly fields you could roll down, and if you concreted them over they would make a great skateboard park.

I stood for while on a tumulus. A tumulus is an ancient burial mound. Some have been there for thousands of years, back to the days of Saxons and Vikings and no telly. It gave me a strange feeling standing there, kind of comforting, like being part of something big, and dying didn't matter. Wow, I thought to myself. This would make a great site for a multi-screen drive-in cinema.

I pressed on to the river. Things got very boggy, so I got on to the road, and stopped at the bridge like the old teacher in my story. There was no sign of the Old Marnover Fly. I reckoned he'd seen me coming and had turned into a chicken.

The other side of the bridge was a steep, steep hill. Half way up it I found a sign thrown into the hedge. The sign said JOIN MARNOVER SCHOOL – A SCHOOL WITH A FUTURE! Fifty metres further on I came across the bedraggled figure of Mr Zinn slumped by the roadside.

'Are you all right, sir?' I asked.

Mr Zinn looked up but hardly seemed to see me. 'A waste of time,' he murmured. 'A total waste of time.'

'Better luck tomorrow, sir,' I said cheerfully.

Suddenly Mr Zinn grabbed me by the shoulders, eyes blazing. 'Tomorrow?' he raged. 'There isn't going to be a tomorrow, if we carry on like this!'

'Er . . . what do you think we should do, sir?' I asked, nervously.

Mr Zinn spoke slowly and gravely, through gritted teeth. 'Fight dirty,' he said.

CHAPTER 9

Breaking the law

I was quite anxious going to school next day. To my surprise, however, Mr Zinn seemed quite calm. He still pumped his squeeze-ball of course, but quite calmly and regularly. Everyone applauded in assembly when Miss Dorrit showed off my graph. Then Mrs Whiffy had an announcement.

'Today,' she said, 'the school football team will play Old Soxtink Juniors.'

This came as a bit of a shock to me. I knew I was good, but not *that* good.

'Mr Zinn will post the team on the notice

board,' added Mrs Whiffy.

Sure enough, that break, the team was up:

Bernadette (Capt.) - Goalkeeper

Oh no! He'd put me in goal!

The team was to meet at three-thirty sharp by the main gate. I was there on the dot, carrying my school-team shirt and shorts, which looked like they'd been around since before the war. I was sure I'd seen them in a photo worn by one of those old people with shiny hair and centre partings.

Mr Zinn had a C-reg. Metro so that's what I was expecting to appear. I was wrong. There was a distant rumble, a grinding of gears, and a forty-seater coach turned into view.

'Do we really need this, Sir?' I asked, as I climbed aboard.

'Tradition,' grunted Mr Zinn.

I didn't argue. There was a strange calm determination about Mr Zinn today. He drove the coach at a steady fifty down the winding country lanes, while ramblers and cyclists and the odd rabbit flung themselves into the ditch to avoid us. Soon the tower of Old Soxtink church came into view, then the school. It was smaller than Bigtown Monster Primary but a lot bigger than Marnover. I was disappointed to see that a complete team of eleven were waiting on the school field.

'Will you be *very* disappointed if we lose, sir?' I asked.

Mr Zinn gazed steadily into my eyes. 'Not at all,' he replied, and that little electric-shock smile flickered his lips.

The game went about as well as I expected. After five minutes we were four-nil down and from then on things got worse. I decided my only hope was to wind them up so they fouled me and got sent off, but I soon ran out of my best insults and my worst ones as well.

By half-time it was 38–0. If this was a story in a book I might have made a miraculous recovery, but as you have no doubt realized, this is a real-life story in which everything is completely true. So there was no fairytale victory – in fact it got worse still. Long before the end Mr Zinn had given up shouting advice, and by the final whistle he had disappeared from the touchline altogether.

Ah well. At least I got an Old Soxtink shirt – or was it an Old Shirtstink sock? I can't remember. What I do remember is Mr Zinn sailing into the changing rooms to congratulate the opposition.

'You must all have some cakes and squash,' he declared.

The Old Soxtink boys were very excited about this. They followed Mr Zinn out of the changing rooms, across the field, over the playground and on to the forty-seater coach. The cakes and squash were laid out on the back seat. They looked suspiciously like the cakes and squash from the first morning of term, but the Old Soxtink boys weren't to know that. They tucked in like they'd never seen cake before.

Meanwhile, Mr Zinn was quietly sliding into the driver's seat.

'Mmm,' went the Old Soxtinks.

VRRRRRRRM! went the engine.

What happened next was a blur. I vaguely remember being yanked into the coach, the door closing, lots of shouting, a squeal of tyres, and a small posse of teachers giving chase. Then there was nothing but the open road, the gentle hills, and eleven very confused boys.

'W-where are you taking us?' they blubbered.

'Where am I taking you?' barked Mr Zinn. 'I'm taking you to your new school!'

Mr Zinn was flushed with the blood of life. Even though we'd lost 78–0, the scent of victory was in his nostrils.

'Tell them how wonderful Marnover School is, Bernie!' he cried.

'Very nice,' I assured them.

'We want to go home!' they wailed.

Outside, I stayed calm. Inside, I was working out how many years I might get for being Mr Zinn's sidekick.

'Aren't you worried about the police, Mr Zinn?' I asked nervously.

'The police?' scoffed Mr Zinn. 'The nearest police station's in Bigtown! They'll never catch us!'

Just then, a big blue tractor rolled out of a field ahead of us and turned into the road. This kind of thing happens in the country. Mr Zinn hit the brakes. The tractor accelerated to its top speed of two miles an hour.

HONK! HONK! went Mr Zinn's horn.

There was no way past, and soon there was no way back. A queue of cars was lined up behind us. There was nothing to do but wait for that police car to arrive from Bigtown.

CHAPTER 10

Detention

The kidnap fiasco had a powerful effect on Mr Zinn. Next morning at assembly he seemed a broken man, with hardly the strength to squeeze his squeeze-ball. No mention was made of the football match, or of the events which took place afterwards. Mrs Whiffy would only talk about good news. She had Mr Stains up on stage to tell us about the tea-towel he'd sold to a woman who sounded suspiciously like my mum. Then Mrs Whiffy talked about new ideas for attracting pupils, ideas which did not involve *breaking the law* or *besmirching the good name of the school.*

Mr Zinn did not look impressed. After assembly I noticed him taking down the wall-display in his room and emptying the tadpole tank down the sink. By breaktime the room was as cold and miserable as the police cell where Mr Zinn had spent the night.

Then, during lunch break, the real drama began. I was playing solo two-ball against the wall of the kitchen when Mrs Whiffy came tearing round the corner, closely followed by Miss Dorrit.

'Where's the fight?' gasped Mrs Whiffy.

'What fight?' I replied.

'The brawl!' gasped Miss Dorrit. 'The horrid brawl!'

I hadn't a clue what they were on about. I may have played myself at footy, but beating myself up was another matter.

'Must be somewhere else,' I said.

Mrs Whiffy hurried off somewhere else, Miss Dorrit hot on her heels. I took up the rear. As we turned the corner of the bike sheds, a disturbing sight came into view. Mr Zinn, red in the face, was eyeball to eyeball with Mrs Floss, who was digging an egg-whisk into his chest. Mr Stains stood nearby, making a lame attempt to keep the peace.

'*Mister* Zinn!' roared Miss Whiffy. 'What on earth is going on?'

'She started it!' barked Mr Zinn.

'Liar!' snapped Mrs Floss.

'Am not!' barked Mr Zinn.

'Are too!' snapped Mrs Floss.

'Be quiet the pair of you!' said Mrs Whiffy. 'And for goodness sake smarten yourselves up!'

Mrs Floss wiped an arm across her nose and Mr Zinn tucked his shirt back in.

'I'll listen to your stories one at a time,' said Mrs Whiffy. 'You first, Mrs Floss.'

'Please, Mrs Whiffy,' replied Mrs Floss, 'I was just walking out of school, minding my own business, when Mr Zinn ran up to me and said . . . a bad word.'

' "Sandwiches" isn't a bad word!' blurted Mr Zinn.

Mrs Floss shrieked.

'Quiet, Mr Zinn!' said Mrs Whiffy. 'You *know* that word upsets Mrs Floss! Why did you say it?'

'Please, Mrs Whiffy,' said Mr Zinn, 'she was laughing at me.'

'I was *not* laughing at you!' blabbed Mrs Floss. 'I was just laughing.'

'Laughing at nothing?' snapped Mr Zinn. 'Then you'd better see a head doctor.'

Mrs Floss whipped her egg-whisk into the air. Mrs Whiffy stepped smartly between them and put on her scariest face.

'What do you think people will say if they find out our staff are fighting?' she roared. 'It will be the end of us!'

'It already is the end,' mumbled Mr Zinn.

'Shut up, Mr Zinn! Now apologize, the pair of you!'

Mrs Floss looked sideways and buttoned her lip. Mr Zinn folded his arms with a stony face.

'Right,' said Mrs Whiffy. 'You leave me no alternative. I am putting you both in detention.'

CHAPTER 11

More problems – and a hairnet

Mr Zinn's old classroom made an excellent detention room. Mr Zinn sat in one corner, Mrs Floss in the other. Neither said a word through the whole afternoon. They still hadn't apologized next morning, and they were sat in exactly the same places at lunchtime.

Now Marnover School had a new problem. Who would cook the dinners? Not Mr Stains – he was too old and doddery to carry hot metal dishes. Not Miss Dorrit – she was teaching me till lunch. Not Mrs Whiffy – she was far too busy, and anyway, she was the Head.

That only left one person. And that person wasn't very happy about it.

'I'm a caretaker,' said Mr Tomsky. 'Not a cook.'

'You are a member of my staff,' said Mrs Whiffy, 'and you'll do as I say.'

'But I don't know how to cook,' said Mr Tomsky. 'I know how to fire boilers, and unlock doors, but I couldn't boil an egg if you paid me.'

'I do pay you,' said Mrs Whiffy, 'and I'm sure you can cook *something*.'

Still Mr Tomsky protested. He said he was an old-fashioned kind of fellow, and cooking was women's work, and anyway, Mrs Tomsky wouldn't let him in the kitchen even if he wanted to go there, which by the way he didn't.

Mrs Whiffy waited till Mr Tomsky finished blithering on, then marched him smartly down to the school canteen. She explained where the ovens were, and what a spatula was, and which can had the cooking oil in it. Then she opened a drawer and took out an old folder called MRS FLOSSES BOKE OF RECIPEES.

'You will cook one of those,' she said.

Mr Tomsky looked around himself like a cat in a new house. He flicked weakly through the recipe book. He seemed to have lost the will to fight.

'One more thing,' snapped Mrs Whiffy.

Mr Tomsky looked up.

'You will have to wear one of these,' said Mrs Whiffy.

Mrs Whiffy held up a hairnet. A pink hairnet.

'You're joking!' gasped Mr Tomsky.

'Health and Safety regulations,' said Mrs Whiffy. 'We don't want the school closed because of poor hygiene, do we?'

That was the last straw for Mr Tomsky. He flatly refused to wear the hairnet. He said he would rather be dangled upside-down in a lake full of crocodiles.

'Well,' said Mrs Whiffy, with a huff. 'We don't have a lake full of crocodiles. But we *do*

have a detention room.'

That afternoon, Mr Tomsky sat half-way between Mrs Floss and Mr Zinn, and the rest of us went hungry. It all seemed kind of stupid to me, especially the bit about the hairnet. After all, Mr Tomsky was as bald as a coot.

CHAPTER 12

The inspectors are coming

Next morning at assembly, Mrs Whiffy put on her gravest face. She had been putting on some pretty grave faces, so you can imagine how grave this one was.

'The inspectors,' she said, 'will arrive in two days' time.'

Mr Stains shook his head sadly. Miss Dorrit looked as happy as ever, almost as if she hadn't heard what Mrs Whiffy said.

'All is not lost,' said Mrs Whiffy. 'I am planning a special Marnover School Lottery. That is sure to attract some pupils.'

Mrs Whiffy explained the lottery. At the beginning of the week every pupil would get a scratchcard. At the beginning of each lesson they could scratch off one number. At the end of the week Mrs Whiffy would announce the winning numbers. The winner would be top of the class and get an A on their report.

'That doesn't seem fair,' I mumbled.

'It isn't fair,' agreed Mrs Whiffy. 'But the purpose of school is to prepare children for Life and Life isn't fair, so we will be doing our job perfectly.'

Miss Dorrit gave a little round of applause. Mr Stains carried on shaking his head. As we filed down to the classroom he seemed slower and wearier than ever. Once or twice I thought he was going to slump to the ground. Somehow he made it to his desk and we began the long and tiresome task of taking the register. Just as he began to carve a little line next to my name, however, he stopped moving altogether.

'Mr Stains?' I asked.

Mr Stains made no reply.

'Shall I get out the pencils?' I asked.

Mr Stains made no movement.

I got up, stood in front of Mr Stains, and waved my hand before his face. Still there was no flicker of life. I thumped the desk. Nothing. My heart began to thump very hard. I trotted, ran, then sprinted to Mrs Whiffy's office.

'Please, Miss,' I gasped, 'Mr Stains isn't moving!'

Mrs Whiffy looked at me doubtfully. 'I hope this isn't an excuse to get you off homework,' she said.

'Honest, Miss!'

Mrs Whiffy put down her scratchcards and followed me to the classroom. She didn't seem too disturbed when she saw Mr Stains sat there like a zombie. She snapped her fingers a few times and peered into his eyes. Then she sighed.

'I should have known this was going to happen,' she said.

Mrs Whiffy explained that Mr Stains was

just moving very, very slowly. He had very little energy, as we all knew, and when he was under stress it almost dried up altogether.

'I shouldn't have told him about the inspection,' said Mrs Whiffy.

'What are we going to do with him?' I asked.

'Well,' said Mrs Whiffy. 'There's really only one place for him.'

CHAPTER 13

A class full of children

It seemed the worse things got, the happier Miss Dorrit became. 'Everything's going to be fine!' she said, when we'd closed the door on Mr Stains, Mr Tomsky, Mrs Floss, and Mr Zinn. 'Everything's going to be fine!' she said again, when Mrs Whiffy told us that the lottery cards had come out printed backwards. 'I will have a class full of children tomorrow!' she said, as the three-thirty bell went.

'You reckon?' I said, not too convinced.

'Oh yes, Bernadette,' she replied. 'I'm quite certain.'

'Really?' I said. 'Why's that?'

'Because the fairies have just told me!' replied Miss Dorrit. Her smile became brighter still and a slightly confused look came into her eyes.

I must admit I didn't have much faith in Miss Dorrit's fairies and I was even less convinced that we would come up with thirty pupils before the inspection.

Imagine my surprise when I walked into school and heard Miss Dorrit addressing a full classroom: 'Royston, will you get away from the window! Yes, very good, Kerry, but it's not what I asked you to do, is it? Blue worksheet, Harvey, not the green one! For goodness sake, Jackie, why didn't you go before the lesson started?'

I pushed open the classroom door.

The room was completely empty.

Miss Dorrit turned to me with a weary smile. 'Goodness, Bernie,' she said. 'I'm beginning to long for the days when it was just you.'

I decided to play it cool. Miss Dorrit might be dangerous. 'Sorry I'm late, Miss,' I said.

'Hurry up and sit down,' said Miss Dorrit.

I moved uncertainly between the desks and chairs. 'Anywhere, Miss?' I asked.

'Anywhere,' repeated Miss Dorrit. 'As long as no one's already sitting there!'

Miss Dorrit shared a chuckle with the phantom class.

Nervously, I slid on to a chair.

'*Oh*, no,' said Miss Dorrit, shaking her head.

'No, Miss?' I replied.

'I'm not having you two sitting together,' said Miss Dorrit.

'Fair enough, Miss,' I replied.

I tried another seat.

'Oh, that *is* nice to see!' exclaimed Miss Dorrit.

'It is?' I replied.

'I thought you two would never make up,' said Miss Dorrit.

I turned to the space next to me, then back to Miss Dorrit. 'It was an argument over nothing, really,' I said.

I've no idea why it occurred to me to say

this, but I soon regretted it.

'And has she given it back to you?' asked Miss Dorrit.

'Er . . . yes, Miss,' I replied.

'Perhaps you'd better hand it to me for safekeeping,' said Miss Dorrit.

Miss Dorrit held out her hand. The air became tense.

'Miss!' I blurted. 'Royston's at the window again!'

It was a flash of genius. By the time Miss Dorrit had given Royston what for, she'd clean forgotten about the unknown thing an unknown girl had given back to me.

'And now . . .' said Miss Dorrit, beaming widely, '. . . it's time to make a wall frieze!'

I kept my job as paint, paintbrush, paper and pencil monitor. I loyally gave out thirty of everything and settled down to make another brilliant self-portrait. Or so I thought, till Miss Dorrit came round to inspect my work.

'No, no, silly!' she said. 'You're not supposed to be painting yourself!'

'Er . . . who do I paint?' I asked, fearing the worst.

'The person opposite!' trilled Miss Dorrit.

This was becoming impossible. I didn't even know if the person opposite was white, black, brown, yellow or sky-blue-pink. I had to find a way out of this classroom.

An idea came to me. I yelled out, 'Ow!' clattered my chair to the floor and went into a furious fist fight with thin air.

'Bernadette!' cried Miss Dorrit.

'He started it!' I yelled.

Miss Dorrit marched down the classroom and pulled me away from the phantom scrapper. 'You will both go to Mrs Whiffy, this minute!' she cried.

'Thanks, Miss,' I replied. I didn't need to be asked twice. I was at Mrs Whiffy's office before you could say Royston Robinson.

'Please, Miss,' I pleaded. 'I think you'd better come and see Miss Dorrit.'

'Miss Dorrit?' queried Mrs Whiffy. 'What's the matter with her?'

'I think she's joined the Monster Raving Loony Party,' I replied.

Mrs Whiffy followed me back to the classroom, where there was a scene of total chaos. Melissa had spilt a glass of water all over Ainsley's painting, Harriet had a nosebleed and Royston had completely ignored Miss Dorrit's warnings and fallen right out of the window.

'Mrs Whiffy!' gasped Miss Dorrit. 'Thank goodness you've arrived!'

Mrs Whiffy, as usual, was calmness itself. She quickly took stock of the situation, walked quietly up to Miss Dorrit and laid a hand on her shoulder.

'We'll give you the rest of the day off, Janet,' she said.

'But . . . my class . . .' spluttered Miss Dorrit.

'They'll be just fine,' said Mrs Whiffy. 'We'll have them working so quietly no one will even know they are there.'

'If . . . you're sure,' replied Miss Dorrit.

'I'm quite sure, Janet,' said Mrs Whiffy. 'Now, if you'll come along with me, I have a

nice quiet room you can sit in.'

Miss Dorrit slipped on her cardigan, picked up her bag and went without further fuss. Mrs Whiffy exchanged a knowing glance with me. It was so reassuring having her there, like a solid rock in the middle of a wild sea. I followed her out, like a chick after a mother hen.

Just as we got to the door, Mrs Whiffy turned to the empty classroom and pointed a dangerous finger.

'And you lot get on with something, *quietly*!' she warned.

CHAPTER 14

Crisis!

Now that the entire staff were in detention, Mrs Whiffy's attitude to me was different. She didn't treat me like a pupil any more. I'd become a kind of deputy. We sat in her office together with tea and biscuits, while she considered the situation.

'We have no pupils,' she began, 'and no teachers. We have no school meals and no heating. Tomorrow morning the inspectors arrive. Would you call this a crisis, Bernadette?'

'Definitely a crisis, Mrs Whiffy,' I replied.

'I thought so,' said Mrs Whiffy.

Mrs Whiffy stood up and began to pace the room. I could tell she was going to do something big and important.

'I am going to show you something very sacred,' she declared.

Mrs Whiffy went to the school safe and unlocked it with an ancient key. Out came a large, musty old book. On the book it said MARNOVER VILLAGE SCHOOL. FOUNDED 1881. HEAD'S LOG.

It seemed a strange kind of log to me, till I saw it was full of writing, and realized it was like the Captain's Log in *Star Trek*.

'This writing,' said Mrs Whiffy, 'is the work of Charles Buckshot, founder of the school and its first Head.'

'He doesn't mind, does he?' I asked. 'I'd die if anyone read *my* diary.'

'Oh no,' said Mrs Whiffy. 'All headteachers of the school are instructed to read the Head's Log. It contains Charles Buckshot's last wishes.'

Mrs Whiffy began to read the log in a solemn voice.

'*Marnover School must remain a school and nothing else. Never must it be allowed to close and re-open as a dogs' home or museum of pig farming. If ever the school should come into crisis, its present headteacher must . . . must . . .*'

Mrs Whiffy's voice trailed away.

'Must what, Miss?' I pleaded, urgently.

'Are you sure you want to hear this?' asked Mrs Whiffy.

'Too right!' I replied.

Mrs Whiffy took a deep breath. *'Must obey the instructions,'* she continued, *'which they will find . . . inside . . .'*

Mrs Whiffy trailed away again. This was driving me mad. 'Inside what, Miss?' I squealed.

'Inside . . .' whispered Mrs Whiffy, *'. . . my secret crypt.'*

The words 'secret crypt' came like a deadly footfall, turning my spine to a quivering column of goo. Our eyes met and held fast.

'So,' I said, as calmly as possible. 'You've got to open his secret crypt.'

'That's right,' said Mrs Whiffy. 'We've got to open his secret crypt.'

'We?' I repeated, noticing the small but important difference between what we had said.

'I've decided to make you my monitor,' explained Mrs Whiffy.

'What about my homework?' I blithered.

'This *is* your homework,' replied Mrs Whiffy.

'What if my mum looks in my homework diary and sees *'Breaking into old headteacher's secret crypt?'* I blabbed.

Mrs Whiffy could tell I was stalling. Her face set hard. She was taking no more nonsense.

'I will be at your gate one hour before dawn,' she said. 'Be ready.'

CHAPTER 15

The secret crypt

I did as I was told. At five in the morning, when everything was silent and cold, I slipped out of bed, put on some dark clothes (for camouflage) and went out to the gate. But please don't follow my example. As I said at the beginning, this story isn't quite *all* true.

Not a soul stirred. I looked to the top of the hill, where Marnover church was a shadow against the sky. The sound of quick footsteps came to my ears. There, at the end of the lane, appeared a small, hurrying figure with two shovels over her shoulder and a briefcase in her other hand. It could only be Mrs Whiffy.

'Ready?' she said, as our eyes met. There was a look of steely resolve on her face.

'Ready,' I replied.

We set off, without further words. We hurried past the shop, the one-pump garage and the village hall. We cast an anxious glance at the vicarage. Then it was the final steep walk up Church Hill, and the gravestones coming into view.

We reached the church gate. Mrs Whiffy unloaded the shovels with a sigh. For the first time I noticed uncertainty on her face.

'All right, Miss?' I asked.

'All right, Bernie,' replied Mrs Whiffy, a little wearily.

'You . . . won't be bothering with the register this morning?'

'Not this morning, no.'

Suddenly a clopping of hooves came to our ears. Mrs Whiffy pushed me into the graveyard. We dived behind a tombstone just as an old painted caravan came into view, pulled by an enormous black horse.

'The knife grinder,' whispered Mrs Whiffy.

The caravan creaked past and off towards the Four Feathers Inn.

'He'll be taking the road to Dogsbottom, no doubt,' whispered Mrs Whiffy.

I didn't ask questions. Things were so weird this morning, the strangest things seemed normal.

'Let's get to work,' said Mrs Whiffy.

We crept between the gravestones to the far side of the church. There, beneath a crooked yew tree, stood a great marble tomb. On it were the words

HERE LIES CHARLES BUCKSHOT
FOUNDER OF MARNOVER SCHOOL
WHO FELL ASLEEP 3RD JANUARY, 1889
REST IN PEACE

By now my heart was beating in double-time. 'You mean . . . they buried him when he was only *asleep?*' I asked with a quiver.

'Of course not!' explained Mrs Whiffy. 'It's just a figure of speech.'

'I see,' I replied.

To be honest I didn't see at all, but the last thing I wanted was an English lesson.

Mrs Whiffy hacked away at a clump of weeds just past the tomb. Slowly, an old stone came to light.

'That's it,' she said. 'The entrance to the secret crypt.'

'Fantastic,' I peeped in a quivering little voice.

'Let's get to work,' said Mrs Whiffy, holding out a shovel. I took the shovel. My hands could barely hold it.

Mrs Whiffy showed me how to jam the shovel under the stone. I did as I was told, like a robot.

'Now *heave!*' commanded Mrs Whiffy.

With that, Mrs Whiffy put all her weight on the other end of the shovel, and I did the same. There was a creak, then Mrs Whiffy's shovel snapped.

Mrs Whiffy went sprawling to the ground. Meanwhile my shovel came up like a catapult

and sent me flying through the air like a drunken goose.

When we eventually shook ourselves down we were amazed to see that the stone had slipped neatly to the side.

On fairy footsteps I crept to the edge of the hole. Slowly, fearfully, I looked inside.

Inside was a box.

'Can we go now?' I asked, hopefully.

'Oh no,' said Mrs Whiffy. 'We must open this box.'

The first fingers of sunlight were creeping on to the edge of the sky. Just as silently, Mrs Whiffy slipped into the secret crypt. I steadied my breath and followed.

The crypt smelt of earth, and gloom, and centuries of sad, sorry lives. It was strangely cold, colder than the air outside.

Mrs Whiffy placed her broken shovel-end under the lid of the box and pushed down till the veins bulged in her forehead. Again, there was a creak, then a gap appeared. Mrs Whiffy got her hands inside it and ordered me to do the same. With one last frenzied effort, we opened the old headteacher's box and stared open-mouthed at the sight within.

'*What is it?*' I hissed.

There was nothing there. Just dozens and dozens of strange sticks – candles, maybe, or big fat Victorian crayons from the oldest days of school.

Mrs Whiffy's voice was softer than whispering grass: 'Dynamite!'

'Dynamite?' I repeated. 'What's that for?'

'What do you think?' asked Mrs Whiffy. She reached up, pulled her teacher's briefcase into the shed, and started loading it with sticks.

'You're not going to blow up the school!' I cried.

'Come on,' said Mrs Whiffy. 'There's no time to lose.'

Mrs Whiffy snapped shut her briefcase. We replaced things as well as we could and set off back into the village. Dawn had broken now and a few people were crawling out of their burrows.

'Morning, Mrs Whiffy!' said the postman. 'That's a lot of marking you've got in there!'

'Morning, Mrs Whiffy!' said the cow farmer. 'What's this, early morning nature ramble?'

Mrs Whiffy smiled politely to everybody, and I said nothing. At first I was thinking, cool! We're going to blow up the school! But as I passed the houses where I took the petition, a terrible feeling of guilt came over me. After all, it was my fault there were no pupils in the school. All right, I didn't want to go there, but I never meant the old place to get blown to smithereens.

The feeling of guilt grew, like a creeping headache, till it filled all of my brain.

At this point I realized I had to save the school.

We reached the gates. Mrs Whiffy's eyes were fixed ahead, like the lights on a runaway train. 'The basement,' she murmured, '… or the roof?'

I jumped in front of her and spread my arms wide.

'Mrs Whiffy,' I said, 'I cannot allow you to do this.'

For a moment Mrs Whiffy was shocked. Then a glare of pure outrage came into her eyes. 'I *beg* your pardon?' she snapped.

My breath came in little pants. My nerve was going fast. Suddenly, I was a naughty little kid outside the Head's office again.

'Mrs Whiffy,' I warbled, 'I am confiscating that dynamite.'

'*Confiscating?*' stormed Mrs Whiffy. 'Pupils don't *confiscate! Teachers* confiscate!'

I held my ground, even if I was quivering like a web in the wind. 'Mrs Whiffy,' I said, 'give me that dynamite *forthwith.*'

I don't know where I got a word like *forthwith* from, but it certainly impressed Mrs Whiffy. She barged past me and sprinted like a hobgoblin. By the time I had followed her into the school she was through the cloakrooms. When I caught sight of her again she was disappearing through the door to the school tower.

I tried the door. She'd locked it!

I listened helplessly to the sound of her footsteps heading up on to the roof. There was no other way up there. Unless . . .

No time to lose. I ran up to the second floor, pulled open a window, and without a second thought climbed out on to the ledge. Down below was a sheer drop to the playground. Up above was the edge of the roof. In between was an old Victorian drainpipe.

I've never liked heights. Then again, how could I be scared of anything after what I'd just been through?

I got a good hold on the drainpipe and began to climb.

The pipe creaked.

My fingers gripped like tiny pythons.

Bit by bit, I made my way up.

At last my head peered over the gutter. There before me stood Mrs Whiffy, holding a stick of dynamite over the school chimney, a lighter in her other hand.

With one last mighty effort, I heaved myself

on to the roof.

'In my hand is a stick of dynamite,' bellowed Mrs Whiffy. She clicked the lighter and a little flame appeared. 'Stay right where you are!'

I stopped dead.

'Now if you just go back down quietly,' she said, 'you can get the staff out of detention. I can set the dynamite properly and no one will get hurt.'

For a moment I wavered. Then I went for it. 'Miss!' I cried. 'Elgin Marble's looking out of the window!'

I don't know where I got that name from, but the fact is, it worked. Mrs Whiffy looked round, and in that split second I pounced. There was a moment of confusion, a puff of chalk from Mrs Whiffy's cardigan, then the lighter was in my hand.

'Bernadette . . .' said Mrs Whiffy in her strictest voice, 'if you don't give back that lighter, I shall . . . I shall . . .'

'What, Miss?' I scoffed. 'Suspend me? Expel me? Put me into detention?'

The game was up for Mrs Whiffy and she knew it. I watched her authority drain away like water down a plughole. I had broken her spell and we were two equal people.

'I think we'd better go down,' I said gently.

Mrs Whiffy went quietly, without a further word. Downstairs the rest of the staff were arriving to continue their detention, and it seemed only natural that Mrs Whiffy should join them. It also seemed natural for me to stand at the front of the class and act like I was in charge.

'Now listen here,' I said. 'I've just saved this school, so you'd better all listen!'

To my amazement no one objected, and Miss Dorrit even started making some notes. My confidence grew.

'*None* of you are responsible enough to be in charge of this school,' I continued, 'so from now on, I'm in charge. Got that?'

There were a few mumbles of 'yes' and even one 'yes, Miss'.

'I can't hear you!' I railed.

This time the 'yes' was quite loud and clear.

'Right,' I said. 'You will get out some books and do some work!'

'What books?' grunted Mr Tomsky.

'Work books!' I replied.

Everyone fished about in their bags. Mr Zinn brought out *KENNETH WOLSTENHOLME'S BUMPER SOCCER ANNUAL 1965*. Mr Tomsky brought out *INSTRUCTIONS FOR THE USE AND CARE OF Z 915B OIL-FIRED BOILER*. All the others found something useful to read except Miss Dorrit, and I lent her a copy of *WRIGGLY PIG* which soon kept her happy.

At last, it seemed, I could sit back and relax. But no sooner had I put my feet up than there was a *RAT TAT TAT* at the door. I opened it to find two smartly-dressed men with clipboards.

In all the excitement I had clean forgotten about the school inspection.

'Can I ask who's in charge here?' asked Inspector A, looking straight over my head at the grown-ups.

'Me,' I replied, tapping his elbow. 'I'm in charge.'

Inspector A looked down at me, then back at the staff. No one disagreed with me. Inspector A seemed a little confused, but pressed on.

'As you know,' he continued, 'this school is required to have at least six pupils in its classes. As this is clearly not the case —'

'Excuse me,' I said.

'Yes?' replied the inspector impatiently.

'There *are* six pupils in the class,' I said.

The inspector didn't seem to get it.

'Can't you count?' I asked.

The inspector glanced again at the six figures before him.

'But these are . . . adults,' he murmured.

'So?' I replied. 'Education's not just for children, you know.'

The inspectors exchanged glances. They couldn't disagree. I began pacing the room, slowly, my hands behind my back.

'My idea of a village school,' I pronounced, 'is a school for the *whole* village. A place where we can all learn together.'

I've no idea who was putting these words into my mouth, but they carried on coming for ten minutes or so, halted only by the occasional round of applause from Miss Dorrit. By the end of it, Inspector B was also giving me a quiet clap. After a pleasant cup of tea made by my tea monitor, Mrs Whiffy, everyone was smiling and laughing, and the future of Marnover Village School was assured.

CHAPTER 16

Mum grants a wish

Once the story broke, there was no way of stopping the papers. The *Daily Wash* and the *Morning Glory* camped out on our doorstep, and the *Evening Gloom* even bugged the cat.

Soon the whole country had heard about Marnover School. Parents from all over wanted to send their kids there, and quite a few wanted to come themselves. A new era had begun, and Marnover decided to celebrate with a carnival. They made me Carnival Queen and put me in a float full of flowers, except I insisted on wearing my jeans and T-shirt. The Marnover

School staff had their own float, Famous Figures From History, and Miss Dorrit dressed as me.

Mum was overjoyed with me. I'd really made her proud. She wrote letters to all our friends and relatives telling them the whole story, except the bit about going into the old headteacher's secret crypt.

Mum was dressed as a fairy godmother at the carnival. After it was over she said she would grant me a wish.

'Anything?' I asked.

'Anything,' she replied.

I sat there in the field, amid the hustle and the bustle, looking out over the corn and the ancient hills, watching the river lazily flow past the farmhouses, the church, and the knife grinder's caravan, as the sun slowly set on the village that had become my home.

'Well?' said Mum.

'Can we go back to Grosshampton?' I asked.

About the author

I was brought up in Southampton and decided to be a writer when I was about five. My newspaper *World Times* was featured on Southern Television when I was nine, and I was very embarrassed about it.

My first novel was published in 1986 and since then I have written about thirty books. I have also had proper jobs, like selling shoes and teaching at university.

The idea for *One Girl School* came from a newspaper story – there really was a village school with one pupil in it. Apart from that, my story is completely made up, and nothing to do with Marnhull, the village where my mum and dad live.